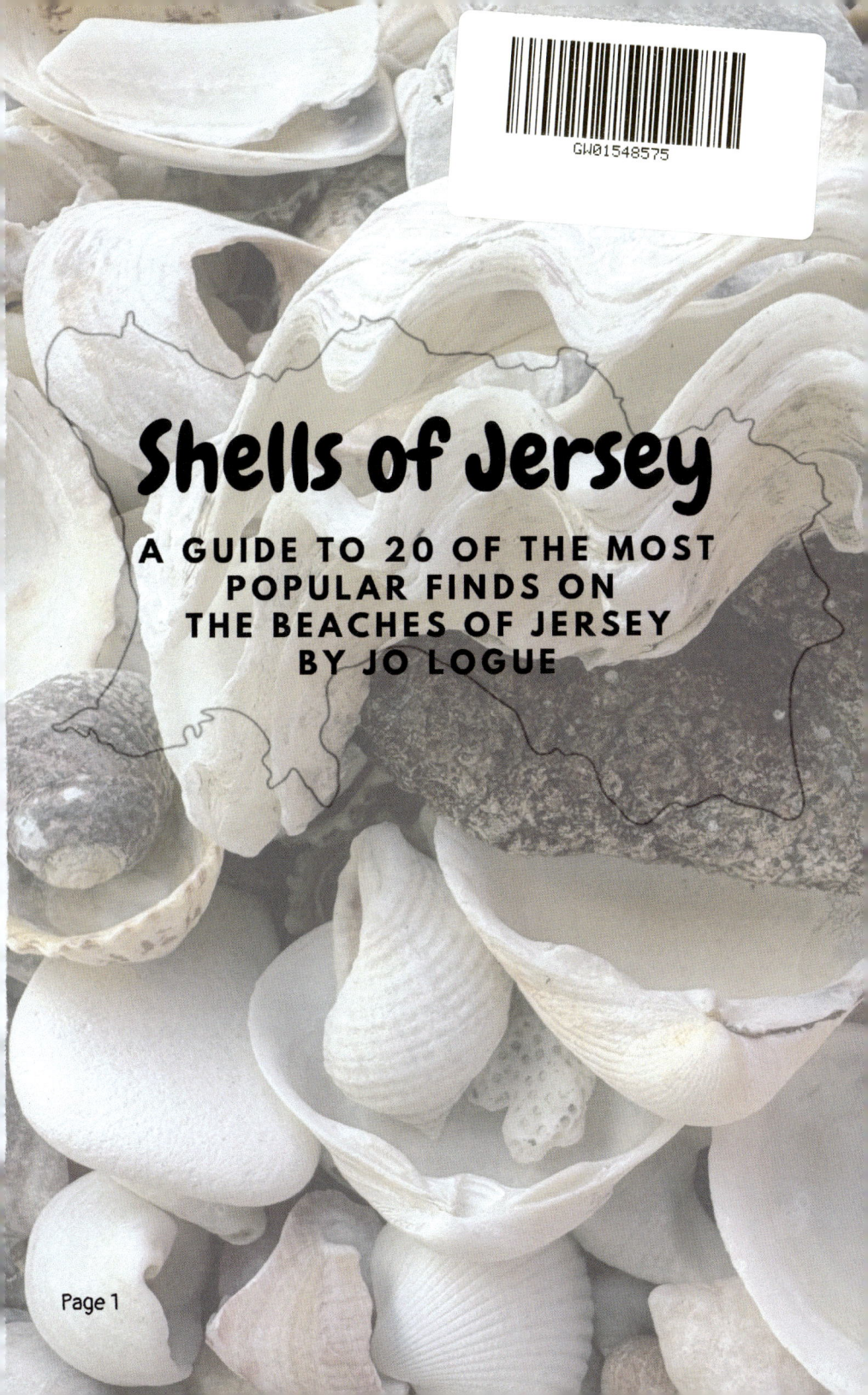

Shells of Jersey

A GUIDE TO 20 OF THE MOST POPULAR FINDS ON THE BEACHES OF JERSEY
BY JO LOGUE

Dedication

For my dad, Frank -
who always saw the beauty in the smallest things,
whose joy at living near the sea was contagious,
who knew so much about the beach and its treasures,
low-water fishing, tide times, and phases,
and who was always eager to share it all.
Thank you for teaching me - and my children -
how to see, to pause,
and to treasure it all.
This book is for you.

Copyright © 2025 Jo Logue
All rights reserved.
No part of this publication may be reproduced, distributed, or transmitted in any form or by any means, including photocopying, recording, or other electronic or mechanical methods, without the prior written permission of the publisher, except in the case of brief quotations embodied in critical reviews and certain other noncommercial uses permitted by copyright law.

Contents	Pages
Welcome to the beach	5
Beachcombing tips	6
Where can I find shells?	7
What is a "Foot"?	8
About the shells	9
The Limpet Shell	10
The Common Cockle Shell	12
The Flat Periwinkle Shell	14
The Dog Cockle Shell	16
The Netted Dog Whelk Shell	18
The Pennant's Topshell	20
The Slipper Limpet Shell	22
The Dog Whelk Shell	24
The Oyster Shell	26
The Common Whelk Shell	28
The Sting Winkle Shell	30
The Razor Clam Shell	32

Contents continued	Pages
The Painted Topshell	34
The Turban Topshell	36
The King Scallop Shell	38
The Mussel Shell	40
The Pullet Carpet Shell	42
The Warty Venus Shell	44
The Cowrie Shell	46
The Common Wentletrap Shell	48
The Ormer Shell	50
The secret world of micro shells	52
What to do with your shells	53
Fun shapes to make with your shells	54
Colouring pages	58
Favourite shells	60
About the Author	62
Well Done Certificate	63

Welcome to the beach!

Walking along the beach is like going on a treasure hunt! You can hear the waves, feel the sand under your feet, and spot special things the sea has left behind, smooth stones, sea glass and drift wood caught against the rocks or mixed in with seaweed and best of all, seashells !

Did you know Jersey has one of the biggest tidal range in the world? When the sea goes out, the island nearly doubles in size- that means even more beach to explore!

Can I keep the shells I find?

Yes, you can keep most of the shells you find on Jersey's beaches!

However , there are exceptions to this, the most notable are:

-Do not take any protected shells, like the Five-shilling Shell.
-Do not collect shells from Portelet Bay's "No Take Zone."

The 20 shells shown in this book (pages 10 to 49) are common types that you are allowed to collect.

The Five-Shilling Shell

Beachcombing tips:

- Look where the tide has been-shells often gather in the ridges of the sand where waves have been lapping and also where waves have pushed them against rocks.
- Gently turn shells over to make sure they're empty.
- Never pull shells off rocks-they're still alive!
- If you move a rock, put it back the same way. Tiny creatures may be living underneath and you shouldn't disturb their home.
- Bring a little bucket or bag for your shells (and maybe a small sieve to find tiny shells mixed in the sand).
- Safety first, be careful-the sea can come back quickly, check the tide times and don't go too far out on the rocks.
- Always stay safe and never go somewhere you might get stuck.
- Take only what you need and always be kind to nature.

Where can I find shells?

Shells can be found on almost all of Jersey's beaches, however some of my best finds have been at the beach at Havre des Pas, where you are likely to find most of the shells in this book on a low tide. The ones I like the best are the bright yellow Flat Periwinkles, they are here in abundance.

St Aubin's Bay also has a huge selection of shells, and is a great spot for large Whelk shells and tiny micro shells.

If the tide is low you can walk out to Seymour Tower at La Rocque and on the way you may be lucky to find banks of shells all piled on top of each other . There is a guide online called "How to walk to Seymour tower" which is very informative.

What is a "Foot"? (It's not what you first thought!)

When I first heard that lots of shell creatures have something called a foot, my imagination went wild! I pictured a tiny little foot poking out of a shell-with wiggly toes, maybe even wearing a miniature flip-flop!

But of course, a shell creature's foot isn't like ours at all.

A foot, in the shell world, is the soft, squishy part of the animal that lives inside the shell. It doesn't have toes, and it's not used for walking like our feet. Instead, it's a kind of strong, stretchy muscle that helps the creature slide along rocks, burrow into the sand, or hold tightly onto things so the waves don't carry it away.

It's more like a built-in tummy-scooter than a foot-and it's super clever!

So if you spot the word foot in this book, you'll now know: no toes involved-just one amazing, slippery, sea-scooting part of a shell creature's body.

About the shells

The next pages show photos and fun facts about 20 of the most common shells you can find on Jersey's beaches. If you go beachcombing and find some shells, have a look through this book to see if they're in here! If you spot one, you can tick the box on its page and write down where and when you found it.

I have written my thoughts about each shell and left a space for you to write what you think .

There are over 100 different types of seashells you could find on Jersey beaches, but this book only includes 20 of them. Don't worry if you find a shell that isn't in the book! You can draw it in the blank spaces at the back, or take a photo and send it to me by email (herdofjersey@gmail.com) and I'll do my best to help you identify it.

The shells are grouped starting with the most common ones I've found on our Jersey beaches, and ending with a few that are a little trickier to spot.

Once you have been on your shell-hunting adventure, you can write your name and the date in the certificate on the last page of this book .

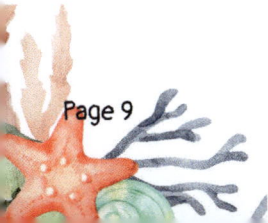

1. The Limpet Shell

Limpets are little sea creatures with cone-shaped shells that stick tightly to rocks. Their shells look like tiny volcanoes! You'll often see them at the beach when the tide goes out. They use a strong foot to hold on tight to rocks so they don't get washed away by the waves.

I have found numerous limpet shells when beachcombing, there is such a variety on the beaches of Jersey, some with deep ridges and dark colours and others smoothed by the sea.

Fun Fact:
Limpets always return to the same spot on the rock after feeding-it's like their own special parking space!

What Jo Thinks: Limpets always make me think of little hats! They look just like the traditional pointy hats some farmers wear when working in the rice fields in Vietnam.

My Thoughts:

The Limpet Shell

I found one ! ☐

Beach:

Date:

2. The Common Cockle Shell

The Common Cockle has a round, ridged shell that looks a bit like a heart if you look at it from the top. It has two matching halves which fit together . It's usually white, cream, or light brown, and sometimes has stripes or pinkish patches.

Cockles live just under the sand in shallow water. They use a tiny foot to burrow down and hide from hungry birds and crabs.

Fun Fact:
Cockles can jump by snapping their shell and using their foot like a spring!

What Jo Thinks : If you find two Cockle Shells still joined together, try opening them like a book-they look just like angel wings!

My thoughts:

The Common Cockle Shell

I found one ! ☐

Beach:

Date:

3. The Flat Periwinkle Shell

Flat Periwinkles are tiny sea snails with smooth, rounded shells that come in lots of colours like yellow, orange, brown, and even green! They look like little seaside sweets . They are about the size of a small marble and love to hide in seaweed on rocky shores. You might spot them clinging to rocks or seaweed, especially when the tide is out, but please only take the shells that are washed up on the sand and are empty.

Fun Fact:
Flat Periwinkles are great climbers! They use their strong foot to crawl up seaweed to find food-and they can even hang upside down without falling!

What Jo thinks :Wow-these are some of my favourite shells! They come in such amazing colours, bright oranges and yellows. They make me smile every time I find them!

My thoughts:

The Flat Periwinkle Shell

I found one !   ☐

Beach:

Date:

4. The Dog Cockle Shell

The Dog Cockle has a strong, chunky shell that is usually creamy, orange, or brown with stripes or wavy lines. It lives buried under the sand and closes its two shell halves tightly to stay safe.

Even though it's called a "dog" cockle, it has nothing to do with dogs-just a funny name!

Fun Fact:
Dog Cockles can live a very long time-some even to 100 years!

What Jo thinks : Isn't it crazy that some Dog Cockles are so old that they may have been around during the Second World War when Jersey was occupied by German soldiers ? While so much was happening above ground, these little creatures were quietly living in the sand .Nature really is amazing!.

My thoughts:

The Dog Cockle Shell

I found one !   ☐

Beach:

Date:

5. The Netted Dog Whelk Shell

The Netted Dog Whelk is a small, sturdy sea snail with a beautifully patterned shell. Its shell is usually pale brown or grey with a crisscross, net-like pattern-hence the name "netted".

These whelks have a long, pointed shell and a short siphon they use to sniff out food. You'll often find them on sandy or muddy shores, especially around the low tide line.

Fun Fact:
The Netted Dog Whelk is like the vacuum cleaner of the seashore! It's a scavenger that uses its keen sense of smell to detect and clean up dead animals buried under the sand-even from several metres away.

What Jo thinks : These shells always remind me of knitted pixie hats-their shape is just perfect!

My thoughts:

The Netted Dog Whelk Shell

I found one! ☐

Beach:

Date:

Page 19

6. The Pennant's Topshell

The Pennant's Topshell has a small, flattish top with lovely pink, purple, and green patterns. It has spiral ridges and a shiny, mother-of-pearl inside and although it is found in Jersey, it's not found on the shores of mainland Britain.

These little shell creatures live on Jersey's rocky shores and in rockpools, where they slowly crawl around eating algae.

Fun Fact:
The Pennant's Topshell has a super strong foot that works like a suction cup! When it feels scared or the tide goes out, it holds on tightly to rocks so it doesn't get washed away or eaten.

What Jo thinks : I often wonder why shells are given the names they have. The Pennant Topshell made me especially curious! it turns out it was named after a man called Thomas Pennant. He lived a long time ago and loved studying animals and nature. Scientists named the shell to remember him and his work. I think that's a lovely way to honour someone who cared about the natural world!

My thoughts:

The Pennant's Topshell

I found one ! ☐

Beach:

Date:

7. The Slipper Limpet

The Slipper Limpet shell is oval and arched, with a distinct white "deck" inside. It can be pale creamy or reddish-brown with blotches of orange or red. Slipper Limpets pile on top of each other in stacks - sometimes five or more! The one at the bottom is usually the oldest and largest (and often female!), while the others above are younger and usually male.

Fun Fact :
Over time, some of the males actually turn into females-how's that for a seaside surprise?

A gentle reminder:
If you spot a stack of slipper limpets on the beach, please don't pick them up. Even if the one at the end looks empty, the others above are probably still alive and snug in their shell homes. It's always best to only collect completely empty single shells that have washed loose from the stack.

What Jo thinks : I think these shells look like sleeping seals which have been known to occasionally visit our Island shores.

My thoughts:

The Slipper Limpet Shell

I found one ! □

Beach:

Date:

8. The Dog Whelk Shell

The Dog Whelk has a twisty, spiral shell that's usually creamy white, grey, or light brown. It can feel bumpy or smooth, and the opening is shaped like a teardrop.

This little sea snail lives on rocky shores and is a clever hunter! It drills tiny holes into other shells to suck out the soft animal inside.

Fun Fact:
Dog Whelks are one of the few sea snails that eat mussels and barnacles!

What Jo thinks: Dog Whelk Shells look like twirly towers-they remind me of the colourful rooftops on a magical castle.

My thoughts:

The Dog Whelk Shell

I found one ! ☐

Beach:

Date:

9. The Oyster Shell

Oyster Shells are rough and bumpy on the outside and smooth and shiny on the inside. They are usually grey, white, or brown, and can be quite heavy. Oysters like to stick to rocks or each other under the sea, forming large groups called "beds".

After a storm you can find beautiful Oyster Shells washed up on the beach at Havre des Pas .

Fun Fact:
Did you know that some Oysters can make pearls? It's their way of protecting themselves when something tiny gets inside their shell! Sadly the Oysters you find on the beaches of Jersey are unable to produce shiny pearls!

What Jo thinks: I love finding shallow Oyster Shells , I paint the rim gold and use them as little trinket dishes for jewellery!

My thoughts:

The Oyster Shell

I found one! ☐

Beach:

Date:

10. The Common Whelk Shell

The Common Whelk has a big, twisty shell with a wide opening and a pointy top. It's usually pale brown, yellow, or grey with rough ridges and spiral lines.

Whelks live in deeper water and crawl along the seabed looking for food like worms, clams, and even dead animals!

Fun Fact:
Whelks lay their eggs in sponge-like yellow cases called "sea wash balls" — you might find them washed up on the beach!

What Jo thinks: Don't you think these shells look like the top of a Mr Whippy ice-cream?

My thoughts:

The Common Whelk Shell

I found one ! ☐

Beach:

Date:

11. The Sting Winkle Shell

Sting Winkles are small sea snails with pointy, spiral-shaped shells. Their shells are usually grey or brown and sometimes have little ridges or bumps. They like to hide in rockpools and under seaweed at low tide.

Fun Fact:
Sting Winkles get their name because they can make a tiny hole in other shells to eat the animal inside-like using a straw for their lunch- that has got to sting!

What Jo Thinks : I think Sting Winkle Shells looks like dragon teeth!

My thoughts :

The Sting Winkle Shell

I found one !

Beach:

Date:

12. The Razor Clam Shell

Razor Clam Shells are long, thin, and curved- a bit like an old-fashioned razor that some barbers still use today . They're usually white, cream, or pale purple, and feel smooth and shiny.

They live buried deep in the sand on flat beaches. The living clam hides inside and can dig very quickly if it senses danger.

Fun Fact:
Razor Clams can dig super-fast- they can disappear into the sand in just a few seconds! They use their strong foot to wiggle down and hide from predators.

What Jo thinks: If you are exploring the beach at very low tide, see if you can spot little keyhole shaped holes in the sand. Sprinkle a pinch of salt in the hole and wait.... if you're lucky a razor fish might pop up, thinking the tide has come in! Be quick though, they're fast at diving back down.

My thoughts:

The Razor Clam Shell

I found one! ☐

Beach:

Date:

13. The Painted Topshell

The Painted Topshell is a beautiful, cone-shaped shell with swirly patterns in pink, purple, green, or yellow. It has fine ridges and a shiny, pearly inside.

These shells are found on rocky shores and in seaweed, where the snail inside grazes on algae.

Fun fact:
The little snail that lives inside the Painted Topshell is just as pretty and colourful as its shell and can be flecked with red, purple or yellow.

What Jo thinks : This shell looks like a swirly slide and I imagine if I was tiny I'd be able to slide down from the top round and round all the way to the bottom !

My thoughts:

The Painted Topshell

I found one !

Beach:

Date:

14. The Turban Topshell

This shell is called a Turban Topshell because it looks a bit like a turban- a type of headwear based on cloth winding. Turban Topshells are strong and rounded, with beautiful spiral patterns on them. Their colours can be creamy white, brown, or even a little bit pink or green and is shiny inside because it's made of a material called mother-of-pearl!
Turban Topshells live at the very low tide mark or below, where they crawl around looking for seaweed to eat.

Fun Fact:
Like many other shells, the Turban Topshell has a little "door" called an operculum that it can close to hide safely inside their shell - like shutting a front door!

What Jo thinks : When I look at the Turban Topshell, it reminds me of a colourful spinning wheel, turning round and round !

My thoughts:

The Turban Topshell

I found one !   □

Beach:

Date:

15. The King Scallop Shell

The King Scallop has two shells which match up and fit together. One shell is flat like the ground and the other is curved like a hill. The Shells are large and have ridges like a fan and can be white, orange or brown. The King Scallop lives on the sea floor and can even swim by snapping its shells together!

Fun Fact:
King scallops have tiny blue eyes all around the edge of their shell to help them spot danger!

What Jo thinks : I love to paint Scallop Shells with bright colours and patterns and use them in displays . I even have a string of them hanging on my garden fence!

My thoughts:

The King Scallop Shell

I found one !

Beach:

Date:

16. The Mussel Shell

Mussels have smooth, shiny shells that are usually dark blue, black, or purple and shaped a bit like a teardrop. They sometimes wash up in big groups, especially near rocks. If you don't find any on the beach, you might spot them on a dinner plate instead! In Jersey, you can eat Mussels in a dish called Moules Marinière-they're cooked in a tasty sauce with garlic and herbs. Lots of people enjoy them as a starter in restaurants.

Mussels live in big clusters on rocks and pier legs, using tiny threads to hold on tight. When the tide is in, they open their shells to feed on tiny bits in the water.

Fun Fact:
Mussels make their own super-strong threads -even stronger than glue!

What Jo thinks : Here's a fun idea. Draw a small circle for a head and a long oval for a body on a piece of paper, like the shape of a dragonfly . Then find 4 Mussel Shells and place them round the body to look like wings ! You can create your own shell dragonfly! (see page 54 for inspiration).

My thoughts:

The Mussel Shell

I found one! ☐

Beach:

Date:

17. The Pullet Carpet Shell

The Pullet Carpet Shell is smooth and oval. It's usually cream, grey, or yellow with wiggly brown or purple lines across it-like a little shell-sized carpet. That's how it got its name!
It likes to hide just under the sand.

Fun Fact:
This shell comes from a clam that's really good at cleaning the sea! It sucks in seawater and filters out teeny-tiny bits of food.

What Jo thinks : This Shell has such a lovely shape. When I look at it, it reminds me of a lady's skirt that flares at the bottom, just like when someone twirls around and their skirt spins out in a big circle!

My thoughts:

The Pullet Carpet Shell

I found one !

Beach:

Date:

18. The Warty Venus Shell

The Warty Venus Shell is a round, chunky shell with little bumps or "warts" on its surface-just like its name says! It can have 20 or more radiating ridges and can be white, yellow, or light brown, and it usually lives buried in sandy seabeds where the water is shallow.

Fun Fact:
Even though it stays hidden under the sand, the Warty Venus Shell has a strong shell to protect it from hungry crabs and fish!

What Jo thinks: When I look at this shell, the little ridges remind me of tiny steps-just like the ones that lead up to an ancient Aztec temple.

My thoughts:

The Warty Venus Shell

I found one ! ☐

Beach:

Date:

19. The Cowrie Shell

This little shell is a Cowrie. It's smooth, shiny, and shaped like an egg. If you turn it over, you'll see a long opening with teeth-like ridges. Cowries use this to protect themselves from hungry predators.

Cowries come in many colours and sizes , but the ones you find on Jersey beaches are small, pale and patterned with all over ridges. I have only found a handful of these pretty little shells whilst beachcombing !

Fun Fact :
Long ago, people used Cowrie Shells like money and also wore them as jewellery for good luck!

What Jo thinks : I think they are happy shells as they look like smiling mouths.

My thoughts:

The Cowrie Shell

I found one ! ☐

Beach:

Date:

20. The Common Wentletrap Shell

The Common Wentletrap has a small, spiral-shaped shell that looks a bit like a twisty staircase or a swirly ice cream cone! The shell is usually white or pale and has lovely ridges that wind all the way around.

Fun Fact:
The name "Wentletrap" comes from a Dutch word that means "spiral staircase"-just like the way the shell curls. Wentletrap Shells were once so rare and loved that people collected them like precious gems !

What Jo thinks : Even though it's called "Common" I've only ever found a couple on our Jersey beaches- so it's actually quite elusive! It will be very special if you find one.

My thoughts:

The Common Wentletrap Shell

I found one ! ☐

Beach:

Date:

The Ormer Shell

I couldn't write a Jersey shell book without mentioning the Ormer Shell.

The Ormer is one of Jersey's most special shellfish. You won't usually find its beautiful shell just lying on the beach as it's only found far out hidden in deep rocky areas in crevices or under boulders. Ormers like to be under the sea, although some may be visible during big spring tides. They prefer to live in areas of high current or turbulence .

The Ormer has a long and fascinating history here on the Island. Ormers are only allowed to be harvested at certain times of year, following old Jersey traditions.

The shell is smooth and flat with a shimmering inside-like a rainbow hidden in stone! People in Jersey have kept Ormer Shells for generations, sometimes using them to decorate boxes or jewellery. I think of it as the crown jewel of Jersey shells.

If you'd like to see an Ormer Shell up close, the best way is to ask a local fisherman or visit the Fish Market-Ormers are a special delicacy in Jersey, and they'll often show you the beautiful shells. You might even spot one in my shop too!

The Ormer Shell

The secret world of micro shells

Sometimes, the tiniest treasures are hiding right under our feet! These teeny-tiny shells are called micro shells, and they're so small you really have to look closely to find them. I like to search for them at St Aubin's Bay, where the sea leaves little ridges of sand after the tide turns.

Look at how tiny these shells are next to a £1 coin! You might find tiny spiral shells or baby cockles. Each one is a perfect little work of art from the sea.

To find these miniature marvels, I use a very fine sieve- it helps me gently sift through the sand and spot shells that are as small as a grain of rice (or even smaller!).I use a pair of tweezers to carefully lift them and put them in a small container.

Fun Fact:
Some sea snails and clams stay tiny their whole lives-just like the micro shells in this picture! Even though they're small enough to sit on a coin, these miniature shells are perfectly formed, with the same spirals and ridges as their larger relatives.

What to do with your shells

If you decide to take some shells with you, it's a good idea to give them a wash when you get home to remove any sand or dirt. I use warm, soapy water. Sometimes little bits of sand hide inside the spiral shells and only fall out after they've dried-so I leave them somewhere warm to dry out properly. Once they're dry, I give them a gentle shake to make sure all the sand has gone from inside. I place the shells in clear glass jars with cork lids so I can see all my favourites together. You can even write a little label for the jar so you will always remember where the shells have come from!

Another fun thing to do is to use your shells to make shapes, like wings, skirts, hats and shoes. I hope the following pages give you some inspiration.

Fun shapes to make with your shells

Use shells to make wings for the insect bodies

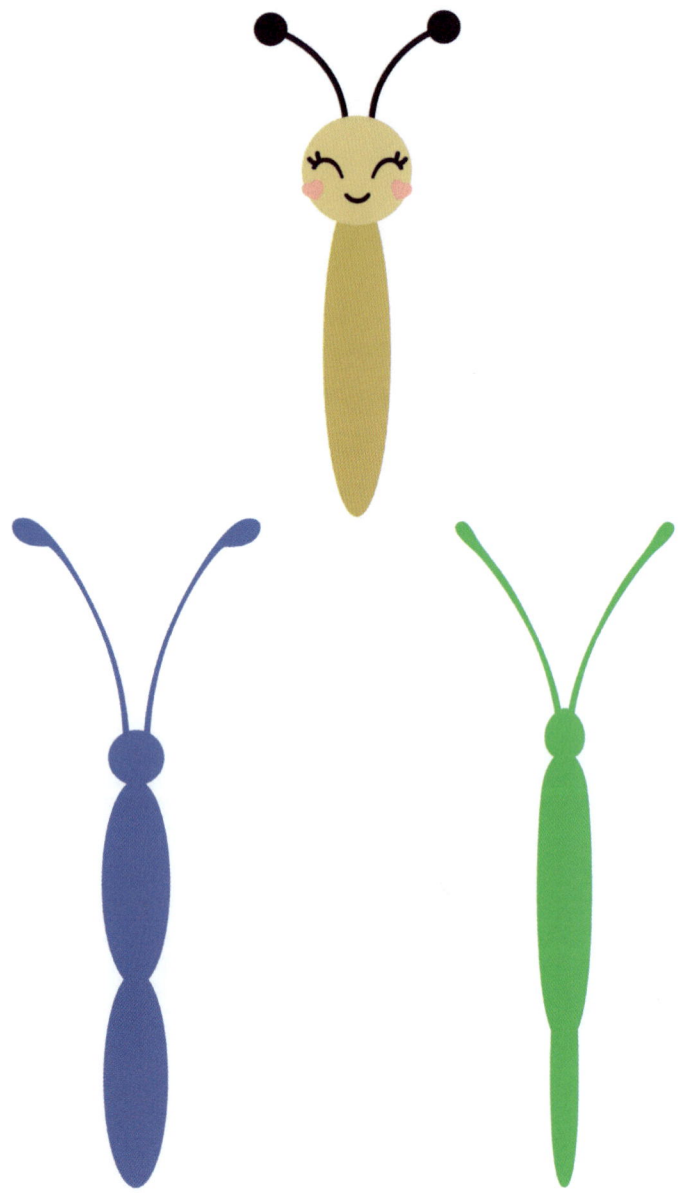

Use shells to make hats and skirts for these ballerinas

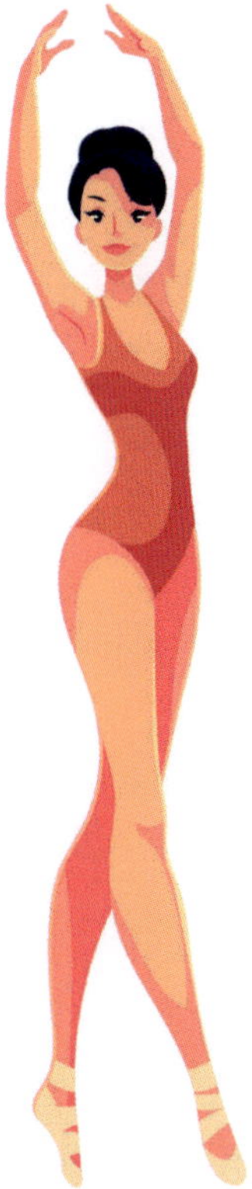

Use shells to make shoes for these feet

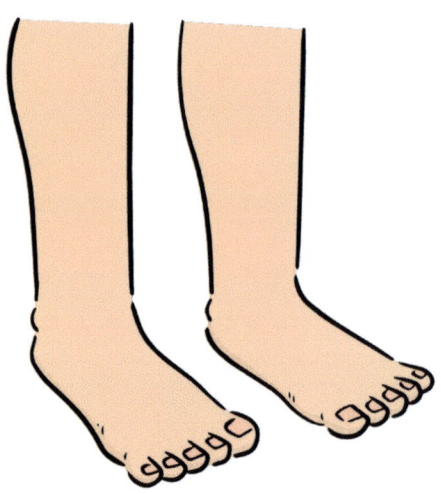

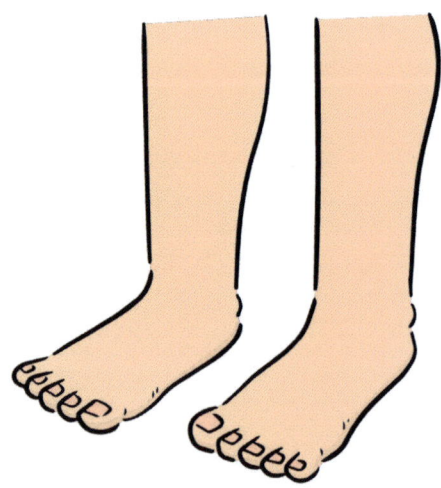

Use shells to make wings for these unicorns

Colouring pages

Favourite shells

Use this space to draw your favourite shells and say what you like about them

Favourite shells

Use this space to draw your favourite shells and say what you like about them

About the Author

I was born and raised on the beautiful island of Jersey, and some of my happiest childhood memories are of days spent on our beaches-collecting shells, peering into rock pools, catching little fish and shrimps with a net, and marvelling at the tiny crabs hidden among the seaweed. I also loved the excitement of going Razor Clam -fishing with my family.

These days, with more time to focus on what I love, I feel incredibly lucky to have turned those early joys into a creative journey. I have a little shop in the Jersey Fish Market where I sell my artwork alongside a carefully curated selection of shells from around the world. You'll also find tiny Jersey shells lovingly displayed in glass jars with cork stoppers-each one a little treasure from our Island shores.

This book is a personal guide, to help children and families learn about the shells they might find on Jersey's beaches. I've done my best to identify each one accurately, and have checked some of the names with the British Shell Collectors' Club.

It's very important to remember that only empty shells should be collected. Taking shells that are still home to living creatures is harmful and should be avoided.

I hope this book brings as much enjoyment to your beach adventures as I've had creating it. Happy Beachcombing!- Jo

Printed in Great Britain
by Amazon